LIFE STORIES

BENJAMIN FRANKLIN

Gillian Gosman

PowerKiDS press™

New York

Published in 2011 by The Rosen Publishing Group, Inc.
29 East 21st Street, New York, NY 10010

First Edition

Editor: Jennifer Way
Book Design: Ashley Burrell and Erica Clendening

Photo Credits: Cover (background, inset), p. 11 iStockphoto/Thinkstock; pp. 4–5, 18 SuperStock/Getty Images; p. 6 Kean Collection/Getty Images; pp. 6–7 Apic/Getty Images; pp. 8–9 FPG/Taxi/Getty Images; pp. 9, 12–13, 17 Hulton Archive/Getty Images; pp. 10, 14 MPI/Getty Images; pp. 13 (inset), 16, 22 (top) Fotosearch/Getty Images; pp. 14–15 Library of Congress; pp. 19, 22 (bottom) Buyenlarge/Getty Images; pp. 20–21 Joseph-Siffred Duplessis/The Bridgeman Art Library/Getty Images.

Library of Congress Cataloging-in-Publication Data

Gosman, Gillian.
 Benjamin Franklin / by Gillian Gosman. — 1st ed.
    p. cm. — (Life stories)
 Includes bibliographical references and index.
 ISBN 978-1-4488-2585-1 (library binding) — ISBN 978-1-4488-2759-6 (pbk.) —
 ISBN 978-1-4488-2760-2 (6-pack)
 1. Franklin, Benjamin, 1706-1790—Juvenile literature. 2. Statesmen—United States—Biography—Juvenile literature. 3. Scientists—United States—Biography—Juvenile literature. 4. Inventors—United States—Biography—Juvenile literature. 5. Printers—United States—Biography—Juvenile literature. I. Title.
 E302.6.F8G677 2011
 973.3092—dc22
 [B]
                                2010036800

Manufactured in the United States of America
CPSIA Compliance Information: Batch #WW11PK: For Further Information contact Rosen Publishing, New York, New York at 1-800-237-9932

CONTENTS

MEET BENJAMIN FRANKLIN

Today most cities have services such as a fire department, a library, and a hospital. The idea for each of these services came from or was greatly helped along by Benjamin Franklin.

Benjamin Franklin lived a long and interesting life. Many of his ideas played an important part in the formation of the United States.

Franklin believed that a community should have services for the common good. This belief became a key idea in the formation of the United States.

Young Ben

Benjamin Franklin was born on January 17, 1706, in Boston, Massachusetts. His father, Josiah, was a candle and soap maker. His mother, Abiah, ran the household, which included 14 other children!

This picture shows Benjamin starting his apprenticeship at his brother James's print shop.

Here is Franklin as an adult in the lab at his home in Philadelphia. Franklin worked on his inventions in his lab.

Throughout his life, Franklin was a writer and an inventor. When he was 12, young Benjamin began an **apprenticeship** under his brother James, a printer. Benjamin even started writing, publishing letters under the fake name Silence Dogood.

LIFE IN COLONIAL AMERICA

Benjamin Franklin's America was a group of 13 **colonies** ruled by Great Britain. In the middle of the 1700s, the American colonists were getting tired of being ruled by Great Britain.

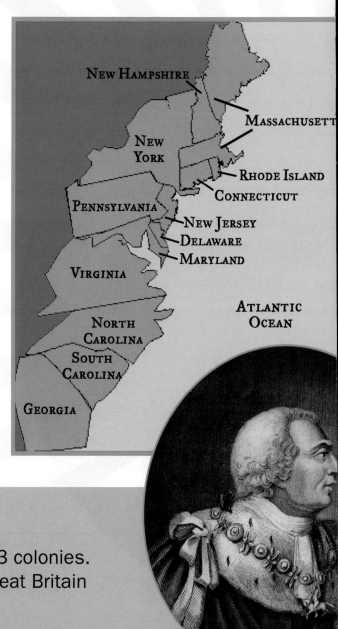

NEW HAMPSHIRE

MASSACHUSETT

NEW YORK

RHODE ISLAND

CONNECTICUT

PENNSYLVANIA

NEW JERSEY

DELAWARE

MARYLAND

VIRGINIA

ATLANTIC OCEAN

NORTH CAROLINA

SOUTH CAROLINA

GEORGIA

Above: This map shows the 13 colonies.
Right: King George III ruled Great Britain and the 13 colonies.

This cartoon shows angry colonists speaking out against taxes that they had to pay to Great Britain.

Great Britain was forcing the colonists to follow laws and pay taxes that did not seem fair to the colonists. Great Britain also decided who would be in charge of the Colonial governments and how court trials would be run.

Making His Way

In 1723, Benjamin Franklin left his apprenticeship with his brother in Boston. He wanted to make his way on his own. He ran away to Philadelphia, Pennsylvania. Philadephia became Frankin's new hometown.

This is Independence Hall, in Philadelphia. Franklin would later be part of the group that met there to write the Declaration of Independence.

This is Franklin's wife, Deborah Read Franklin.

In 1726, Franklin began a self-improvement plan. He took notes on his self-improvement. In 1730, Franklin married Deborah Read. They would raise three children together.

Super Citizen!

Benjamin Franklin took being a **citizen** seriously. He wanted to make Philadelphia a better place.

In 1732, Franklin began printing *Poor Richard's Almanack*. This magazine was

Here Franklin is flying a kite during a thunderstorm to learn about lightning and electricity.

known for its funny sayings. He also formed one of the first fire-fighting companies in America and the Pennsylvania Hospital.

This is the *Poor Richard's Almanack* from 1744.

Franklin was active in both city and Colonial government. In 1753, he was given the job of deputy postmaster for all the colonies.

Franklin also spoke out about the colonies' part in the **French and Indian War**. He spoke

This painting shows a battle of the French and Indian War. The war lasted from 1754 until 1763.

Franklin made this famous cartoon to get the colonies to work together during the French and Indian War.

V.

M.

N.J.

N.Y.

N.E.

OIN, or DIE.

out about Great Britain's treatment of the colonies, too. In 1757, he was picked to be the Pennsylvania Colony's agent, or representative, in London. He held the job until the 1770s.

AMERICA AT WAR

By the 1770s, the American colonists were unhappy with British rule. Living in London, Franklin worked to defend Colonial interests. Great Britain would not change the way it governed the colonies. The colonists were ready for war.

The American Revolution began on April 19, 1775, with the Battle of Lexington and Concord, shown here.

Franklin returned to Philadelphia from London soon after the American Revolution started.

The **American Revolution** began in 1775. Franklin returned to Philadelphia and became Pennsylvania's representative in the **Continental Congress**. This governmental body led the colonies to **independence**.

THE NEW UNITED STATES

Benjamin Franklin played a big part in forming the new United States. In 1776, he helped write the **Declaration of Independence**.

In this painting, Franklin (left) works on the Declaration of Independence with John Adams (center) and Thomas Jefferson (right).

Franklin got France to help the colonies fight Great Britain in the American Revolution. This picture shows him in France.

In 1779, Franklin was named U.S. **ambassador** to France. He held the job until 1785, when he returned to the United States and helped write the **Constitution**.

A Long and Great Life

Benjamin Franklin died on April 17, 1790. He was 84 years old. He was a writer who spoke his mind on the politics of his day.

Franklin was both a world traveler and a man who worked to make his community better. His work can be seen today in the presence of libraries and other public services in every community.

During his life, Franklin was a scientist, an inventor, a politician, and a writer.

TIMELINE

January 17, 1706

Franklin is born.

1718

Franklin begins his printing apprenticeship.

1732

Franklin starts *Poor Richard's Almanack*.

April 17, 1790

Franklin dies.

1779

Franklin is named U.S. ambassador to France.

1757

Franklin is given the job of Colonial agent in London.

Glossary

ambassador (am-BA-suh-dur) Someone who speaks for his or her country.

American Revolution (uh-MER-uh-ken reh-vuh-LOO-shun) Battles that soldiers from the colonies fought against Britain for freedom, from 1775 to 1783.

apprenticeship (uh-PREN-tis-ship) A period in which a young person works with another person to learn a skill or trade.

citizen (SIH-tih-zen) A person who is born in or has a right to live somewhere.

colonies (KAH-luh-neez) Places where people move that are still ruled by the leaders of the country from which they came.

Constitution (kon-stih-TOO-shun) The basic rules by which the United States is governed.

Continental Congress (kon-tuh-NEN-tul KON-gres) A group, made up of a few people from every colony, that made decisions for the colonies.

Declaration of Independence (deh-kluh-RAY-shun UV in-duh-PEN-dints) An official announcement signed on July 4, 1776, in which American colonists stated they were free of British rule.

French and Indian War (FRENCH AND IN-dee-un WOR) The battles fought between 1754 and 1763 by England, France, and Native Americans for control of North America.

independence (in-dih-PEN-dents) Freedom from the control of other people.

Index

Web Sites

Due to the changing nature of Internet links, PowerKids Press has developed an online list of Web sites related to the subject of this book. This site is updated regularly. Please use this link to access the list:
www.powerkidslinks.com/life/franklin/